bottoms up

bottoms up

a cheeky look at life

edited by sean keogh

Published in the United States in 2006
by Tangent Publications
an imprint of
Axis Publishing Limited
8c Accommodation Road
London NW11 8ED
www.axispublishing.co.uk

Creative Director: Siân Keogh
Editorial Director: Anne Yelland
Designer: Simon de Lotz
Production Manager: Jo Ryan
Production Controller: Cécile Lerbiere

ISBN 1-904707-32-7

9 8 7 6 5 4 3 2 1

Printed and bound in China

about this book

A witty look at some of life's absurdities and quirkier moments, *Bottoms Up* teams a selection of quotes and phrases with a collection of amusing animal photographs to make readers smile, laugh, and generally feel better when life is getting them down.

This is an ideal gift book or impulse buy to keep to hand for those moments when life is making you want to scream. Reach for *Bottoms Up* and put the smile back on your face.

about the author

Sean Keogh has worked in publishing for several years, on a variety of books and magazines covering a wide range of subjects. From the many hundreds of contributions that were sent to him, he has selected those that are the wittiest and cheekiest for this collection.

Life is a football game with everyone offside and no referee.

This would be really funny
if it weren't happening
to me.

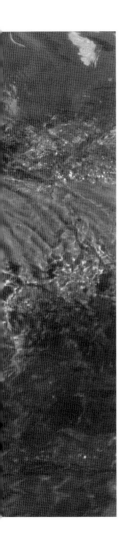

The colder the X-ray table, the more of your body is required on it.

A day without sunshine is, like, night.

The early bird gets the worm…

…the second mouse gets
the cheese.

The good things
that come to those
who wait are the things
those who got there
first didn't want.

My programs don't have bugs…

…they have random features.

If you're still talking about yesterday, you haven't done much today.

Chopsticks: Easy to play on the piano, difficult to eat with.

Whoever said you can't buy happiness had never been shopping.

People who think
they know everything
are annoying those
of us who do.

The good old days…

…when beer was frothy and water wasn't.

How did the fool and his money get together in the first place?

I thought I had made a mistake,
but I was mistaken.

According to my calculations, the problem doesn't exist.

Very funny, Scotty.
Now beam me up my clothes.

If you don't like the way I drive, stay off the sidewalk.

There are two rules in life: Look after number one, and remember your number.

Laughing stock: Cattle with a sense of humor.

Generally speaking,
you don't learn much when
your mouth is open.

According to my
best recollection,
I don't remember.

Anyone who said there is no such thing as a stupid question never worked in customer sales.

If you think things can't get any worse, you have no imagination.

The reason people get lost in thought is that it's unfamiliar territory.

You can't be late until
you show up.

I took an IQ test and the results came back negative.

Life is an endless struggle, but eventually you find a hair stylist you like.

Don't sweat the petty things, don't pet the sweaty things.

If you think no-one cares about you, try missing a couple of car payments.

Dinner is ready when the smoke alarm goes off.

The problem with political jokes is that they get elected.

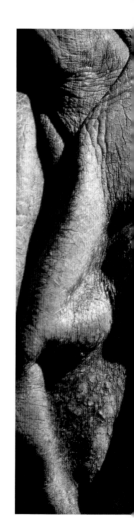

The reason I talk to myself
is that I'm the only one
whose answers I accept.

Learn from the mistakes
of others…

…you won't live long enough
to make them all yourself.

If at first you don't succeed, cheat until caught, then lie.

Anyone can face a crisis—
it's day to day living that
grinds you down.

If you look like your
passport photo,
you definitely need
the vacation.

I think, therefore I am…

…not related to you.

For every action,
there is an equal and
opposite criticism.

The sooner you fall
behind, the more time
you have to catch up.

There's a time and place for everything. It's called college.

I haven't lost my mind…

… it's backed up on disk somewhere.

Never interrupt someone
who is making a mistake.

Diplomacy is the art of saying "Nice doggie" while looking for a bigger stick.

To err is human, but
if the eraser wears out
before the pencil, you're
overdoing it.

Five days a week my body is a temple. The other two, it's an amusement park.

If everything's going really well, you've overlooked something.

Cheer up, the worst is still to come.

Keep smiling…

…it makes people
wonder what you're up to.

A consultant is someone who takes a subject you understand and makes it confusing.

First get the facts straight,
then you can distort them as
much as you like.

Where there's a will, there are five hundred relatives.

Politics: A combination of "poli" meaning many, and "tics" meaning irritating little bugs.

If I explained it to you,
your brain would explode.

There are few personal problems that can't be solved with a suitable application of high explosive.

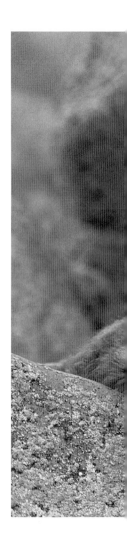

Don't meddle in the affairs of dragons: to them you are crunchy and taste good with ketchup.

If at first you don't succeed, look in the trash for the instructions.

If you can't convince
them you're right,
try confusing them.

A conclusion is where
someone got tired
of thinking.

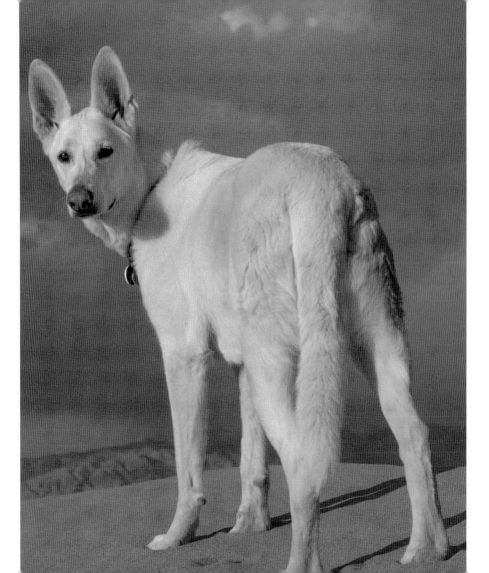

Committee: A group of the unwilling, picked from the unfit, to do the unnecessary.

I wanted to be somebody, but should have been more specific.